Today is a great day!

Bobbie Kalman

🌿 **Crabtree Publishing Company**

www.crabtreebooks.com

Created by Bobbie Kalman

**Author and
Editor-in-Chief**
Bobbie Kalman

Reading consultant
Elaine Hurst

Editors
Kathy Middleton
Crystal Sikkens

Design
Bobbie Kalman
Katherine Berti

**Production coordinator
and Prepress technician**
Katherine Berti

Photo research
Bobbie Kalman

Photographs by Shutterstock

Library and Archives Canada Cataloguing in Publication

Kalman, Bobbie, 1947-
    Today is a great day! / Bobbie Kalman.

(My world)
ISBN 978-0-7787-9506-3 (bound).--ISBN 978-0-7787-9531-5 (pbk.)

    1. Optimism--Juvenile literature. 2. Attitude (Psychology)--Juvenile
literature. 3. Positive psychology--Juvenile literature. I. Title.

BF698.35.O57K34 2011   j158.1   C2010-901973-3

Library of Congress Cataloging-in-Publication Data

Kalman, Bobbie.
 Today is a great day! / Bobbie Kalman.
    p. cm. -- (My world)
 ISBN 978-0-7787-9531-5 (pbk. : alk. paper) -- ISBN 978-0-7787-9506-3
(reinforced library binding : alk. paper)
 1. Optimism in children--Juvenile literature. 2. Attitude (Psychology)--
Juvenile literature. 3. Positive psychology--Juvenile literature. I. Title.
II. Series.

 BF698.35.O57K35 2011
 646.7--dc22

                                                    2010011300

Crabtree Publishing Company

Printed in China/072010/AP20100226

www.crabtreebooks.com   1-800-387-7650

**Published in Canada
Crabtree Publishing**
616 Welland Ave.
St. Catharines, Ontario
L2M 5V6

**Published in the United States
Crabtree Publishing**
PMB 59051
350 Fifth Avenue, 59th Floor
New York, New York 10118

**Published in the United Kingdom
Crabtree Publishing**
Maritime House
Basin Road North, Hove
BN41 1WR

**Published in Australia
Crabtree Publishing**
386 Mt. Alexander Rd.
Ascot Vale (Melbourne)
VIC 3032

Words to know

dancing   family   friends   ice cream

school   smile   team

walk

weather

3

When I wake up
every day,
I feel happy
when I say,

"Today is a great day!"

Today is a great day!
I know good things
are coming my way.

5

Today is a great day!
I **smile** at all the people I see.
They smile right back at me.

My **friends** like my smile and say,
"Yes, today is a great day!"

Today I am playing with my **team**.
"Go, team, go!" we yell and scream.

After the game,
we eat **ice cream**.
Today is a great day!

I learn many new things at my **school**.
I think my school is really cool!
Today is a great day!

Today is a great day!
My friend and I
are **dancing**.
We dance
this way.

Today is a great day!
My whole **family** is out for a **walk**.
While we walk, we laugh and talk.

My family and I have fun together.
We play outside in any **weather**.
Today is a great day!

Activity

When you wake up each and every day, say to yourself, "Today is a great day!" When your day is great, your friends will see how very happy you all can be!

Being kind to yourself is a good start.

Being kind to others opens your heart.

Show your love in every way,

and every day will be as great as today!

Notes for adults

Objective
- to promote positive thinking
- to promote positive behavior toward others
- to help children learn to read by using rhyming words

Before reading the book
Write each of the following words on a blank flashcard:
day, say, today, way; see, me, be; team, scream, ice cream; school, cool; walk, talk; together, weather; start, heart
Keep the rhyming cards together.

Read the book to the child or class
As you read each page of the book, hold up the cards with the rhyming words and ask the children to choose the correct word that will finish each sentence.
Example: "Today is a great... (day).
I know good things are coming my... (way)."
Hold up the words "day" and "way" and ask the children to choose which finishes each of the two sentences.
Do this with each set of cards.

Discussion
Ask the children how thinking that "today is a great day" will help them feel more positive and happy. What could they do at home to make sure they have a great day? Here are some suggestions to brainstorm with them:
- Eat a healthy breakfast. Eating a good breakfast will help them have the energy and brain power to have a great day at school.
- Brush their teeth and hair and wash their hands and faces to feel clean and fresh.
- Listen to some music they like to lift their spirits and move their bodies. Taking a short walk or doing a dance will make them feel awake.
- Hug someone. Giving hugs will make them feel loving.
- Put on some clothes they like. Feeling good about how one looks can make a person feel confident.
- Think of ways they can help others.

Extension: Start with your heart!
"What is the difference between being kind to yourself and being selfish?"
"How can you be kind to yourself?" (see above)
Name five ways you can show others that you care about them. (sharing, saying kind things to others, not hurting the feelings of others, not gossiping, not bullying, having empathy for others, and saying "Today is a great day!" to everyone you meet.)

For teacher's guide, go to www.crabtreebooks.com/teachersguides